Easy as apple pie

Easy as apple pie

Just like
I make!

Caroline Barty

BARRON'S

First English edition for North America published by
Barron's Educational Series, Inc., 2004.

First published by **MQ Publications Limited**
12 The Ivories, 6-8 Northampton Street, London, England

Editor: **Tracy Hopkins**
Design: **Lindsey Johns**

All inquiries should be addressed to:
Barron's Educational Series, Inc.
250 Wireless Boulevard
Hauppage, New York 11788
http://www.barronseduc.com

International Standard Book No. 0-7641-5721-3
Library of Congress Catalog Card No. 2003107442

Printed and bound in China
9 8 7 6 5 4 3 2 1

Contents

Introduction

The humble pie might have been overlooked in recent years in favor of trendier food but it's now due for a revival. There is no better example of a nation's food than its national pie, from the American classic cherry pie to the English crumble to the French tarte Tatin.

We live in an age of convenience food where some can barely wait for the ping of the microwave and the idea of *baking* is up there with going to the dentist. OK, your precious time and waistline may not be able to cope with a pie a day, but I urge you to set aside a couple of hours a weekend to bake a delicious pie. Pie-making is also a great way to introduce your children to baking, so get the kids involved with rolling out the pastry for small individual pies and rediscover the joy of baking together.

Once you become familiar with pastry, you will soon realize just how easy it is to make any of the pies in this book. The gasps of delight from friends and family when they see your efforts will spur you on to try more and more dishes. It's time to shake the dust off the rolling pin and get baking!

The Basics

When following any recipe, it is important to remember a few basic rules. Always read the whole recipe before you start to ensure you have all the equipment and ingredients you need. Use the best ingredients you can find and take care to weigh them out accurately using a set of measuring spoons. The golden rule for successful pastry-making is to keep everything cool—the dough, the work surface, the utensils, and even your hands.

Pie Pans and Dishes

When deciding on which pan to use it is best to be led by the recipe. For an open pie or tart, recipes usually call for a metal loose-bottomed tart pan. These are generally favored above china ones because they conduct heat more efficiently—the last thing you want is soggy, undercooked pastry! Loose-bottomed pans also allow the pie to be transferred easily onto a serving plate, which makes it a lot easier to cut slices. It's also worth investing in good old-fashioned shallow and deep pie dishes. The gentle sloping sides make lining the dishes easy and the pastry won't slip down if you're blind baking. You'll be amazed at how many more pies you make if you have the right dishes! Finally remember that if you change the dish size from the recipe you will have to adjust the cooking times: a smaller, deeper pie will take longer to cook than a shallow, wide one.

Pastry Methods: Manual vs. Food Processor

Throughout this book you will find different methods for making pastry. Some require the rubbing-in method, others tell you to use the food processor. If you don't like getting your hands dirty you can use the food processor all the time but, to my mind, the best, lightest pastry is made by the hands-on method. The main thing to remember is to keep the butter and water cold and not to overwork the dough. Go easy when adding the water—too much and you will end up with tough pastry. You can tell how much water to add by feeling the texture of the dough. Having said that I have great pastry success with KitchenAid machines and the old fashioned Kenwoods. On the slowest settings and with the paddle attachment these machines gently mix and work the dough to produce great results.

Rolling Out Techniques

This is often the part that puts people off making their own pastry. The first thing to remember is to rest the dough—nine times out of ten if someone is having trouble rolling out pastry it is because they skipped the resting period. Resting is essential as the gluten in the flour reacts with liquid and becomes elastic and pliable over time. This will make the pastry easier to roll out and less liable to tear or crumble. Wrap the pastry in plastic wrap and leave in the fridge for at least 20 minutes. When you take it out of the fridge allow it to rest at room temperature for 5 to 10 minutes to soften a little. I favor a heavy, wide wooden rolling pin without handles, about 16 to 18-in. (41 to 46-cm) long. Shape the dough with your hands into the shape of the pan you are using. So if you are using a rectangular pan roughly shape the dough into a rectangle—this just makes it easier to roll out into the right proportions. Don't turn the pastry during rolling—there is a chance it will tear and shrink too much.

Baking Blind

This is the term used when a pie crust is pre-cooked before it is filled to produce a crisp shell. Even if you are going on to cook the filling, it is advisable to bake blind to prevent a soggy crust. Double-crust pies are rarely baked blind because the filling usually requires lengthy cooking and a softer crust is desired. To bake blind, cover the uncooked pie shell with crumpled waxed paper and pour over ceramic baking beans, which conduct the heat and weigh down the pastry. If you don't have baking beans, dried beans or rice work well. When the pastry is firm to the touch and lightly browned remove the paper and beans and continue to cook for a further 4 to 5 minutes to dry out the base.

Shortcrust Pastry: The Basic Method

Making shortcrust pastry is very straightforward and just takes a little practice. Use this method where indicated throughout the book, and see the individual recipes for ingredient quantities.

1 Sift the flour into a mixing bowl with the salt. Add the butter and using your fingertips, rub the butter into the flour until the mixture resembles coarse bread crumbs.

2 Add cold water and using your hands, a narrow spatula, or palette knife, start to bring the dough together, adding a little more water, if necessary.

3 Turn the dough onto a lightly floured surface and knead briefly, just until the dough is smooth. Form into a neat ball, flatten into a disk, and wrap in plastic wrap. Chill at least 20 minutes.

4 Remove the pastry from the fridge and leave at room temperature for 5 to 10 minutes. Unwrap and place on a lightly floured surface. Lightly flour the top of the dough and a rolling pin. Begin rolling the dough by exerting pressure on the rolling pin while rolling it back and forth. Try not to stretch the dough by pulling— allow the weight and pressure of the pin to roll the dough.

5 Roll the pastry to the required size on a lightly floured surface. Gently roll the pastry onto the rolling pin, then unroll it over the pan or dish to cover. Carefully press the pastry in place, removing any overhanging dough with a knife.

6 Prick the base all over with a fork, being careful not to make holes right through the dough. This prevents the dough rising in the middle during blind baking. Chill 20 minutes.

Shortcrust Pastry: Using a Food Processor

If you would prefer to use a food processor to make your shortcrust pastry, rather than the recommended basic method, follow these alternative instructions.

1 Put the flour and salt into a food processor with the butter. Process until the mixture resembles coarse bread crumbs.

2 Add the water to the food processor and, using the pulse button, bring the dough together just until it forms a ball on the blade. You may need to add a little more water.

3 Follow steps three to six of the basic method (above) to finish.

Open
Cooked
Pies

Georgia Pecan Pie

This well-known pecan dessert is best served with a generous dollop of whipped cream or ice cream.

Serves 8–10

1¹/2 cups (175 g) all-purpose flour, plus
   extra for dusting
3 oz. (75 g) cream cheese, softened
¹/2 cup (120 g) butter, softened
2 tbsp. sugar
whipped cream or ice cream,
   to serve (optional)

Filling
3–3¹/2 cups (450–525 g) pecan halves
3 eggs, lightly beaten
1 packed cup (200 g) dark brown sugar
¹/2 cup (125 ml) corn syrup
grated peel and juice of ¹/2 lemon
4 tbsp. butter, melted and cooled
2 tsp. vanilla extract

1 To make the pastry, sift the flour into a large bowl. Add the cream cheese, butter, and sugar and rub with your fingertips until the mixture resembles fine bread crumbs. Form the dough into a ball, then flatten and wrap in plastic wrap; refrigerate 1 hour.

2 Roll out on a lightly floured surface and carefully line the bottom and sides of a 9-in. (23-cm) tart pan. Crimp the edge and refrigerate.

3 Pick out 1 cup (150 g) perfect pecan halves and set aside. Coarsely chop the remaining pecans.

4 To make the filling, whisk together the eggs and brown sugar until light and foamy. Beat in the corn syrup, lemon peel and juice, melted butter, and vanilla extract. Stir in the chopped pecans and pour the mixture into the tart pan.

5 Set the pie on a baking sheet and carefully arrange the reserved pecan halves in concentric circles on top of the egg-sugar mixture.

6 Bake in a preheated oven 350°F (180°C, Gas 4) until the filling has risen and set and the pecans have colored, 45 minutes. Transfer to a wire rack to cool to room temperature. Serve with whipped cream or ice cream, if desired.

The El Paso Diablos Baseball Club in Texas has held the world record for the **largest pecan pie ever made** since 1999. The enormous dessert weighed more than 40,000 pounds and was 50 feet in diameter! The record was previously set at the Annual Pecan Festival in Okmulgee, Oklahoma.

Coffee and Walnut Pie

If you like pecan pie, you'll love this coffee-maple-walnut alternative.

Serves 4–6

scant 3/4 cup (175 g) all-purpose flour
pinch of salt
1/3 cup (75 g) cold unsalted butter, diced
2–3 tbsp. cold water
whipped cream or ice cream, to serve

Filling
scant 3/4 cup (175 ml) maple syrup
1 tbsp. instant coffee granules
1 tbsp. boiling water
2 tbsp. butter, softened
scant 1 cup (175 g) soft light brown
   sugar
3 eggs, beaten
1 tsp. vanilla extract
generous 2/3 cup (115 g) walnut halves

1 Make the pastry following the instructions on pages 10–11.

2 Roll out the dough to line a 9-in. (23-cm) loose-bottomed tart pan. Prick the base and chill 10 minutes.

3 Line the pie shell with waxed paper and weigh down with baking beans.

4 Bake in a preheated oven to 400°F (200°C, Gas 6), about 12 minutes. Remove the paper and beans and return to the oven until pale golden, 10 minutes. Let cool on a wire rack.

5 Reduce the oven temperature to 350°F (180°C, Gas 4).

6 To make the filling, heat the maple syrup in a saucepan until almost boiling.

Dissolve the coffee granules in the boiling water and stir into the maple syrup. Set aside until just warm.

7 Mix the butter with the brown sugar until light and fluffy, then gradually beat in the eggs. Add the warm maple syrup mixture along with the vanilla extract and stir well.

8 Arrange the walnut halves in the bottom of the pie shell then carefully pour in the filling. Transfer to the oven and bake until browned and firm, 30 to 35 minutes. Let cool about 10 minutes. Serve with cream or ice cream.

Coffee is one of the oldest known stimulants. Legends say it was discovered in 800 B.C. by an Ethiopian goatherd, who noticed that his animals became much livelier after eating some unusual red berries. Whatever the truth of the legend, the beans were regularly being boiled and drunk in Arabia by the 9th Century as a drink called *gahwa*, which literally means "that which prevents sleep." Coffee came to Europe, and then America, in around the 16th century by way of Arabian pilgrims and traders.

Gypsy Tart

This traditional British dish is the ultimate butterscotch tart. It's also incredibly tasty and very easy to make. If you are really short of time use ready-made shortcrust pastry.

Serves 8

generous 2 1/2 cups (300 g) all-purpose flour
2 tbsp. confectioners' sugar
3/4 cup (175 g) cold unsalted butter, diced
1 egg yolk
2–3 tbsp. cold water

Filling
1 2/3 cups (400 ml) evaporated milk
1 3/4 cups (340 g) soft dark brown sugar

1 Make the pastry following the instructions on pages 10–11, adding the confectioners' sugar with the flour. Whisk the egg yolks with the cold water. Make a well in the center of the flour and pour in the egg mixture.

2 Roll out the pastry to line a deep 9-in. (23-cm) loose-bottomed tart pan. Prick the pastry and chill 10 minutes.

3 Line the pie shell with waxed paper and weigh down with baking beans. Bake in a preheated oven 400°F (200°C, Gas 6) until golden and crisp, 20 to 25 minutes. Remove the paper and beans and reduce the oven to 350°F (180°C, Gas 4).

4 Place the evaporated milk and brown sugar in a large mixing bowl and whisk with a hand-held electric mixer until thick and frothy, 10 to 15 minutes. Pour the mixture into the pie shell and bake 15 to 20 minutes. Don't worry if it doesn't look set—it will when chilled. Let cool completely and chill.

Raspberry and Coconut Pie

Children will love a slice of this pie and it's especially good for lunch boxes or picnics.

Serves 8

2¹/4 cups (250 g) all-purpose flour
pinch of salt
¹/3 cup (75 g) cold unsalted butter, diced
2 oz. (50 g) vegetable shortening
2–3 tbsp. cold water

Filling
³/4 cup (175 g) unsalted butter
³/4 cup (175 g) sugar
3 eggs, beaten
10 oz. (275 g) shredded coconut
4 tbsp. raspberry jelly

1 Make the pastry following the instructions on pages 10–11, adding the vegetable shortening with the butter.

2 Roll out the pastry to line a rectangular 12 x 8-in. (30 x 20-cm) loose-bottomed tart pan. Prick the base with a fork and chill 10 minutes.

3 To make the filling, whisk the butter and sugar until light and fluffy. Slowly beat in the eggs and fold in the coconut.

4 Spread the jelly over the pastry base and spoon the coconut mixture on top, levelling out the surface.

5 Bake in a preheated oven 375°F (190°C, Gas 5) for 35 to 40 minutes. Let cool a little and cut into slices.

Rich Chocolate Tartlets

**These little tarts are filled with a
wonderful light chocolate mousse.
Serve as a special treat with cream.**

Serves 6

2¹/2 cups (275 g) all-purpose flour
pinch of salt
4 tbsp. (25 g) confectioners' sugar
³/4 cup (175 g) unsalted butter, diced
2 egg yolks
4 tbsp. cold water

Filling
4 oz. (115 g) bittersweet chocolate,
   at least 50% cocoa solids, broken
   into pieces
2 eggs
1¹/2 tbsp. sugar
¹/2 cup (125 ml) heavy cream

1 Make the pastry following the
instructions on pages 10–11, adding the
confectioners' sugar with the flour. Whisk
the egg yolks with the cold water. Make
a well in the center of the flour and pour
in the egg mixture.

2 Divide the pastry into six pieces. Roll
out each piece thinly on a lightly floured
surface and line six individual tartlet pans.
Prick the bases and chill 10 minutes.

3 Line each pie shell with waxed paper
and weigh down with baking beans.
Bake in a preheated oven 400°F (200°C,
Gas 6) until golden and slightly crisp, 15
minutes. Remove the paper and beans
and return to the oven, 5 minutes.

4 Reduce the oven temperature to
375°F (190°C, Gas 5).

5 To make the filling, melt the chocolate
in a bowl set over a saucepan of
simmering water. Let cool slightly.

6 Whisk the eggs and sugar together in
a separate bowl until pale. Whisk in the
cream then the melted chocolate. Pour
the chocolate batter into the pie shells
and bake until set, 15 minutes.

Cheese Tartlets

The filling for these individual tartlets is a kind of light cheesecake mixture enhanced with lemon peel. They are best served warm.

Makes 6

scant 1 cup (110 g) all-purpose flour
pinch of salt
5 tbsp. (75 g) cold unsalted butter, diced
2 tbsp. sugar
1/2 beaten egg
1 tbsp. cold water
confectioners' sugar, for dusting

Filling
1 cup (120 g) cottage cheese
3 egg yolks
2 tsp. grated lemon peel
1 tsp. vanilla extract
1/3 cup (75 g) sugar
4 tbsp. heavy cream

1 Make the pastry following the instructions on pages 10–11, adding the sugar with the flour. Whisk the egg yolks with the cold water. Make a well in the center of the flour and pour in the egg mixture.

2 Roll out the pastry on a lightly floured surface to line six deep brioche pans and trim off any excess. Prick the bases and chill 10 minutes. Line each one with waxed paper and weigh down with baking beans. Bake in a preheated oven 400°F (200°C, Gas 6) until golden and crisp, 15 minutes. Remove the paper and beans and return to the oven, 5 minutes.

3 Reduce the oven temperature to 325°F (160°C, Gas 3). To make the filling, put the cottage cheese, egg yolks, lemon peel, vanilla extract, and sugar in a bowl and whisk together until smooth. Lightly whisk in the cream until smooth.

4 Pour the mixture into the pie shell. Bake until lightly set, 25 to 30 minutes. Let cool slightly then serve dusted with confectioners' sugar.

Curd or cottage cheese was the standard type of cheese eaten around the world for centuries. It was originally made by souring milk, but is now made from drained and pressed milk curds. Legends say that **cheese was accidentally discovered** by an Arabian merchant when the milk he was carrying in a pouch on his camel was separated into curds and whey by a combination of the heat, the movement of the camel, and the enzymes in the lining of his pouch!

Honey and Mixed Nut Tart

Shortcrust pastry is really versatile. Here, it encases a delicious honey and nut filling.

Serves 8

1¹/2 cups (175 g) all-purpose flour
pinch of salt
6 tbsp. (90 g) cold unsalted butter, diced
2–3 tbsp. cold water
heavy cream, to serve

Filling
¹/3 cup (75 g) unsalted butter
1 cup (250 ml) honey
2¹/3 cups (350 g) mixed nuts, such as
    pecans, walnuts, hazelnuts, and
    almonds

1 Make the pastry following the instructions on pages10–11.

2 Roll out the dough to line a 9-in. (23-cm) loose-bottomed tart pan. Prick the pastry and chill 10 minutes.

3 Line the pie shell with waxed paper and weigh down with baking beans. Bake in a preheated oven to 400°F (200°C, Gas 6), about 12 minutes.

4 Remove the paper and beans and return to the oven until golden, 10 minutes. Let cool on a wire rack.

5 Reduce the oven temperature to 375°F (190°C, Gas 5).

6 To make the filling, melt the butter and honey in a medium saucepan over low heat. Increase the heat and let bubble until starting to darken, 1 to 2 minutes. Stir in the nuts and return the mixture to simmering point. Remove from the heat and let cool slightly.

7 Transfer the mixture to the pie shell. Return to the oven and bake until the nuts are golden and fragrant, and the pastry is nicely browned, 5 to 7 minutes. Serve warm with cream.

Chocolate and Pecan Pie

The pie is filled with a deliciously fudgy mixture of nuts, chocolate, and maple syrup. Delicious warm or cold with a dollop of whipped cream.

Serves 8–10

2 cups (225 g) all-purpose flour
pinch of salt
4 tbsp. (25 g) confectioners' sugar
1/2 cup (120 g) unsalted butter, diced
2–3 tbsp. cold water

Filling
1 1/2 cups (225 g) pecans
5 oz. (150 g) bittersweet chocolate,
  roughly chopped
4 tbsp. (55 g) unsalted butter, diced
3 large eggs
generous 1 cup (225 g) soft light brown
  sugar
3/4 cup (185 ml) maple syrup
1 tbsp. all–purpose flour

1 Make the pastry following the instructions on pages 10–11, adding the confectioners' sugar with the flour.

2 Roll out the pastry to line a 10-in. (25-cm) loose-bottomed tart pan. Prick the base and chill 10 minutes.

3 Line the pie shell with waxed paper and weigh down with baking beans. Bake in a preheated oven, 350°F (180°C, Gas 4) until golden and crisp, 20 minutes. Remove the paper and beans.

4 Reduce the oven to 325°F (170°C, Gas 3). Roughly chop three-quarters of the pecans with a large knife and scatter over the cooked pastry case.

5 Melt the chocolate and butter in a saucepan set over a pan of simmering water or microwave on medium, 2 minutes. Stir and let cool.

6 Whisk together the eggs, brown sugar, and maple syrup. Stir in the cooled chocolate and fold in the flour. Pour into the pastry case. Arrange the remaining nuts on top and bake until the center is just set, 50 to 55 minutes.

Lemon-Lime Meringue Pie

Tangy, sweet, and delicious, this deep frothy pie will have everyone coming back for more. It's good served chilled too!

Serves 6–8

2¹/₂ cups (275 g) all-purpose flour
pinch of salt
4 tbsp. (25 g) confectioners' sugar
³/₄ cup (175 g) unsalted butter, diced
2 egg yolks
4 tbsp. cold water
confectioners' sugar, for dusting

Filling
grated peel and juice of 3 lemons
grated peel and juice of 3 limes
generous ²/₃ cup (150 g) sugar
5 tbsp. cornstarch
4 tbsp. (55 g) butter
5 egg yolks

Meringue
5 egg whites
1¹/₄ cups (275 g) sugar
¹/₂ tsp. vanilla extract
1 tsp. cider vinegar
1 tsp. cornstarch

1 Make the pastry following the instructions on pages 10–11, adding the confectioners' sugar with the flour. Whisk the egg yolks with the cold water. Make a well in the center of the flour and pour in the egg mixture.

2 Roll out the pastry on a lightly floured surface to line a deep 9-in. (23-cm) loose-bottomed tart pan. Prick the base and chill 10 minutes.

3 Line the pie shell with waxed paper and weigh down with baking beans. Bake in a preheated oven 400°F (200°C, Gas 6) until golden and slightly crisp, 15 minutes.

Remove the paper and beans and return to the oven, 5 minutes.

4 Reduce the oven temperature to 300°F (150°C, Gas 2).

5 To make the filling, combine the lemon and lime juices in a measuring pitcher to a scant 1 cup (225 ml), adding water if necessary. Pour into a saucepan with the peel, a scant 1 cup (225 ml) water, and sugar. Heat gently to dissolve the sugar.

6 Mix the cornstarch with 5 tbsp. cold water. Whisk the mixture into the juice. Continue whisking gently until thickened, then whisk in the butter and egg yolks. Bring to a boil over low heat, whisking all the time, then simmer, 3 minutes. Remove from the heat and set aside to cool slightly. Pour into the pie shell.

7 Whisk the egg whites until they form soft peaks. Gradually whisk in the sugar until stiff and glossy. Blend the vanilla extract, vinegar, and cornstarch together and fold into the meringue.

8 Place spoonfuls of the meringue over the lemon-lime filling. Bake until lightly golden, 40 to 50 minutes. Let cool, 20 minutes, before serving.

Pumpkin Pie

Pumpkin pie has been a favorite since colonial days and this sweet, spicy tart is a must at Thanksgiving. It tastes best served warm with light cream.

Serves 6–8

3 cups (350 g) all-purpose flour
pinch of salt
1/4 cup (25 g) confectioners' sugar
1 cup (225 g) cold unsalted butter, diced
2 egg yolks
4 tbsp. cold water
light cream, to serve

Filling
1 1/2 lb. (675 g) pumpkin purée
2 eggs, beaten
scant 1/2 cup (90 g) soft brown sugar
1 cup (250 ml) corn syrup
1 cup (250 ml) heavy cream
2 tsp. ground cinnamon
1 tsp. ground dried ginger
1/2 tsp. ground nutmeg
1 tsp. vanilla extract

1 Make the pastry following the instructions on pages 10–11, adding the confectioners' sugar with the flour. Whisk the egg yolks with the cold water. Make a well in the center of the flour and pour in the egg mixture.

2 Roll out the pastry to line a 9 1/2-in. (24-cm) loose-bottomed tart pan. Prick the pastry and chill 10 minutes.

3 Line the pie shell with waxed paper and weigh down with baking beans. Bake in a preheated oven 375°F (190°C, Gas 5) until golden and crisp, 20 minutes. Remove the paper and beans and let cool on a wire rack.

4 For the filling, put the pumpkin purée into a large mixing bowl. Add the eggs, brown sugar, syrup, and cream and mix well. Stir in the spices and vanilla extract. Spoon the mixture into the pie shell and bake in a preheated oven 375°F (190°C, Gas 5) until the filling is firm to the touch, 30 to 35 minutes. Serve warm with very cold light cream.

MORTON PUMPKIN FESTIVAL

Morton, Illinois calls itself the "Pumpkin Capital of the World" because it processes over 85% of the world's canned pumpkin. Every September since 1967, the town has celebrated its beloved vegetable at the annual Morton Pumpkin Festival, which features a huge parade, live music, a carnival, and even a soap box derby.

The Festival pays tribute to all the traditions associated with the pumpkin—from carving scary faces into them at Halloween to eating pumpkin pies to celebrate the harvest at Thanksgiving—through a variety of contests and festivities. Events include the Pumpkin Weigh-In, which has prizes for the tiniest pumpkin as well as the largest, and the traditional Pumpkin Carving Contest. The cooking contests give participants the chance to showcase their favorite pumpkin dishes, with recipes ranging from conventional pumpkin pies and desserts to all manner of unusual appetizers, entrees, and "miscellaneous" pumpkin dishes.

The ever-popular "Punkin Chuckin" contest is another not-to-be-missed event in Morton. Adult and youth teams compete to design and build a huge array of catapults, air cannons, and other creative contraptions, solely for the purpose of hurling 10-pound pumpkins the farthest!

"Pumpkin pie, if rightly made, is a thing of beauty and a joy—while it lasts... a perfect pumpkin pie, eaten before the life has gone out of it, is one of the real additions made by American cookery to the good things of the world."

The House Mother

Pear Frangipane Tart

A rich, buttery almond tart which is delicious served warm or cold with whipped cream.

Serves 8

2¹/₂ cups (275 g) all-purpose flour
¹/₄ cup (25 g) confectioners' sugar
³/₄ cup (175 g) unsalted butter, diced
2 egg yolks
4 tbsp. cold water
confectioners' sugar, for dusting
whipped cream, to serve

Filling
³/₄ cup (175 g) unsalted butter
³/₄ cup (175 g) sugar
1¹/₂ cups (180 g) ground almonds
2 eggs, beaten
a few drops almond extract (optional)
14-oz. (400-g) can poached pears in
    syrup, drained (about 6 halves)
1 oz. (25 g) sliced almonds

1 Make the pastry following the instructions on pages 10–11, adding the confectioners' sugar with the flour. Whisk the egg yolks with the cold water. Make a well in the center of the flour and pour in the egg mixture.

2 Roll out the pastry to line a 9¹/₂-in. (24-cm) loose-bottomed tart pan. Prick the pastry and chill 10 minutes.

3 Line the pie shell with waxed paper and weigh down with baking beans. Bake in a preheated oven 375°F (190°C, Gas 5) until golden and crisp, 20 minutes. Remove the paper and beans and reduce the heat to 350°F (180°C, Gas 4).

4 To make the filling, whisk the butter and sugar until pale and fluffy, then mix in the ground almonds. Gradually whisk in the eggs and the almond extract, if using.

5 Spoon the mixture into the pie shell and level out. Arrange the pear halves on top of the mixture, pressing them down lightly. Scatter over the almonds. Bake for 55 minutes to 1 hour.

6 Remove from the oven and let cool 10 minutes. Dust with confectioners' sugar just before serving with whipped cream.

Pears have been popular for centuries, although it is not known exactly where or when they were first cultivated. The Greek poet Homer called the fruit "a gift of the gods" and **the Romans are said to have developed more than 50 varieties of pears** before introducing them to the rest of Europe. There are now more than 5,000 different varieties of pears grown all over the world, but mainly in Italy, China, and North America.

Crumble-Topped Blueberry Pie with Cinnamon Pastry

This twist on the classic British crumble dessert features a cinnamon pastry case and delicious blueberry filling. Serve the pie warm or cold with whipped cream.

Serves 6–8

2 cups (225 g) all-purpose flour
pinch of salt
1 tsp. ground cinnamon
1/2 cup (120 g) unsalted butter, diced
3–4 tbsp. cold water
whipped cream, to serve

Filling
11/2 lb. (675 g) blueberries
1/3 cup (75 g) sugar

Crumble topping
11/2 cups (175 g) all-purpose flour
pinch of salt
1/2 cup (120 g) butter, diced
1/3 cup (70 g) light soft brown sugar
generous 1/2 cup (75 g) sliced almonds

1 Make the pastry following the instructions on page 11, adding the cinnamon with the flour.

2 Roll out the dough to line a 9-in. (23-cm) loose-bottomed tart pan. Prick the pastry and chill 10 minutes.

3 Line the pie shell with waxed paper and weigh down with baking beans. Bake in a preheated oven 400°F (200°C, Gas 6), about 12 minutes.

4 Remove the paper and beans and return to the oven until pale golden, 10 minutes. Let cool on a wire rack.

5 Mix the blueberries and sugar together and set aside.

6 To make the crumble topping, put the flour and salt into a large bowl. Add the butter and rub into the flour until coarsely combined, with largish lumps of butter still showing. Stir in the brown sugar.

7 Spoon the blueberries into the pie shell and top evenly with the crumb mixture. Sprinkle over the sliced almonds.

8 Transfer to the oven and bake until golden and bubbling, 20 to 25 minutes.

The blueberry is the quintessential American fruit— a real favorite in all sorts of classic American desserts and one of the country's most popular berries. Blueberries were a significant part of the Native Americans' diets when the first settlers arrived. The colonists also began to eat the small wild berries in large quantities, adding them to soups and stews, as well as pies, and even using them in some medicines.

MACHIAS WILD BLUEBERRY FESTIVAL

Washington County, Maine produces 85% of the world's blueberries, which the locals celebrate at their annual Machias Wild Blueberry Festival. Alongside the parades, concerts, sports, games, and cookery contents, they also hold their infamous Blueberry Pie Eating Contest!

The turnout is always huge, and the fun tremendous as people of all ages compete to eat an entire two-crust blueberry pie in just sixty seconds— without using their hands! It's not as easy as it sounds. All are welcome to join the feast, but remember to wear an old shirt or a large napkin as you could end up wearing more of your pie than you eat!

Blueberry Streusel Tart

This has to be one of the best blueberry recipes there is—tucked under the almond streusel topping, the berries stay beautifully succulent. You can use blackberries, currants, or gooseberries instead of blueberries. Adjust the sweetness as necessary, and add a little grated orange peel if liked.

Serves 8

2/3 cup (150 g) butter, softened
3 tbsp. sugar
1 egg
2 cups (225 g) all-purpose flour
1/4 cup (60 ml) light cream
1/2 tsp. vanilla extract
2 tbsp. ground almonds
2 tbsp. soft white bread crumbs
crème fraîche or plain yogurt, to serve

Filling
1 lb. 9 oz. (700 g) blueberries
1/2 cup (120 g) sugar
5 tbsp. soft white bread crumbs
3 tbsp. sliced almonds
2 tbsp. light brown sugar
1/2 tsp. ground cinnamon

1 To make the pastry, beat the butter and sugar together in a bowl until light and fluffy. Beat in the egg with a little of the flour. Stir in the remaining flour alternately with the cream and vanilla extract, mixing to make a smooth, soft dough.

2 Spoon the dough into a greased 101/2-in. (26.5-cm) tart pan, then use your fingers to gently ease it evenly over the bottom and up the sides of the pan. Mix the ground almonds and bread crumbs together, and sprinkle the mixture evenly over the bottom of the pie shell.

3 To make the filling, mix the blueberries with the sugar and half the bread crumbs. Spoon the mixture into the pie shell.

4 Mix the remaining bread crumbs with the sliced almonds, brown sugar, and cinnamon in a bowl. Scatter the mixture evenly over the blueberries.

5 Bake in a preheated oven 400°F (200°C, Gas 6) until the pastry is cooked and the streusel topping is golden, 30 minutes. Serve warm or cold, with crème fraîche or yogurt.

Open Uncooked Pies

Mississippi Mud Pie

This rich dessert was among Elvis Presley's favorites, and, appropriately, it originated in the state where he was born.

Serves 8

6 tbsp. butter, softened
1 cup (120 g) all-purpose flour
2 tbsp. ice water
1/2 cup (60 g) chopped walnuts
cocoa powder and chopped nuts,
   to decorate

Filling
1 cup (120 g) confectioners' sugar
18 oz. (500 g) cream cheese, softened
2 cups (500 ml) heavy cream, whipped
1 x 6-oz. (450 g) package instant
   chocolate pudding mix
4 cups (1 liter) milk
1 heaped tsp. cocoa powder

1 Rub the butter and flour together with your fingertips until the mixture resembles fine bread crumbs. Stir the water and walnuts into the mixture until evenly distributed. Press the mixture into a 9-in. (23-cm) pie pan.

2 Bake the base in a preheated oven 350°F (180°C, Gas 4) for 12 to 15 minutes. Remove from the oven and let cool.

3 In a separate bowl, combine the confectioners' sugar, cream cheese, and half of the cream, reserving the rest for the topping. Gently spread the mixture over the cooked base and chill.

4 In a bowl, prepare the chocolate pudding mix using the milk, according to the packet instructions. Mix in the cocoa powder. Spread the chocolate pudding mix over the chilled pie.

5 Top with the remaining whipped cream, dust with a fine layer of cocoa powder, and sprinkle with chopped nuts. Refrigerate for 4 hours before serving.

Marshmallow and Chocolate Pie

This is similar to a rich cheesecake but with a difference—it has a tempting marshmallowy filling with a creamy layer of chocolate. Sumptuous!

Serves 8–10

6 oz. (175 g) graham crackers, crushed
   to fine bread crumbs
generous 1/3 cup (85 g) unsalted butter,
   melted

Filling
scant 2 2/3 cups (580 g) cream cheese
1/2 cup (120 g) sugar
1 tsp. vanilla extract
3 eggs, beaten
2 egg yolks
4 oz. (115 g) mini marshmallows

Topping
1 1/4 cups (300 ml) heavy cream
5 oz. (150 g) milk chocolate, broken into
   small pieces

1 Mix the graham crackers with the melted butter and press into the bottom of a 9-in. (23-cm) springform cake pan. Chill for 30 minutes until firm. Wrap the outside of the pan in aluminum foil.

2 To make the filling, mix together the cream cheese, sugar, and vanilla extract. Beat in the eggs and egg yolks then fold in the marshmallows. Spoon the mixture into the cake pan and level the top.

3 Place the pie in a roasting pan half-full of boiling water and bake in a preheated oven 350°F (180°C, Gas 4) for 50 minutes. Let cool, then chill 2 to 3 hours until firm.

4 To make the chocolate topping, bring the cream up to boiling point in a saucepan. Take off the heat and stir in the chocolate until smooth. Let cool 10 minutes then pour the sauce over the pie and chill until the chocolate has set.

Dark Chocolate and Toffee Tart

A richly indulgent tart, this is pure pleasure when served with a spoonful of fresh cream.

Serves 6–8

2 1/2 cups (275 g) all-purpose flour
pinch of salt
4 tbsp. (25 g) confectioners' sugar
3/4 cup (175 g) unsalted butter, diced
2 egg yolks
4 tbsp. cold water

Filling
1/2 cup (125 ml) water
1 1/2 cups (350 g) sugar
1/2 cup (125 g) corn syrup
generous 1 cup (240 g) unsalted butter
1 cup (250 ml) heavy cream
1 tsp. vanilla extract
4 oz. (115 g) bittersweet chocolate, at
    least 50% cocoa, grated

1 Make the pastry following the instructions on pages 10–11, adding the confectioners' sugar with the flour. Whisk the egg yolks with the cold water. Make a well in the center of the flour and pour in the egg mixture.

2 Roll out the pastry to line a 9 1/2-in. (24-cm) loose-bottomed tart pan. Prick the pastry and chill 10 minutes.

3 Line the pie shell with waxed paper and weigh down with baking beans. Bake in a preheated oven 375°F (190°C, Gas 5) until golden and crisp, 20 minutes. Remove the paper and beans and let cool.

4 To make the filling, place the water in a large saucepan. Add the sugar and syrup, and cook over low heat until the sugar has dissolved. Increase the heat and bubble about 10 minutes, until the sauce is a deep caramel color.

5 Add half of the butter together with the cream and vanilla extract and stand back—it will bubble up. Stir until the mixture is smooth. Pour into the pie shell and chill 2 hours until set and firm.

6 Melt the chocolate with the remaining butter in a heatproof bowl set over a saucepan of barely simmering water. Let stand, 15 minutes.

7 Pour the chocolate mixture over the top of the tart, spreading it evenly with a narrow spatula. Chill at least 1 hour to set before serving.

Chocolate is a gift from the heavens according to Mayan and Aztec Indian legends! The Aztecs made hot bitter drinks from the beans of the *Theobroma cacao* tree, which means "food of the gods." They believed that drinking their *chocolatl* would give them wisdom and power. Europe was not introduced to the Aztec's chocolate drink until the late 16th century when it was brought to Spain and sweetened with sugar. Chocolate continued to undergo changes for many years, but it was not mixed with milk to create the popular modern milk chocolate until the late 18th century.

Ice Cream Pie

Vanilla and chocolate ice cream make the best filling for this luscious pie, but you can substitute these for your favorite flavors.

Serves 6–8

6 oz. (175 g) chocolate chip cookies, crushed
generous 1/3 cup (85 g) unsalted butter, melted

Filling
3 cups (750 ml) vanilla ice cream, slightly softened
3 cups (750 ml) chocolate ice cream, slightly softened
5 oz. (150 g) milk chocolate, broken into pieces
2 tbsp. (25 g) unsalted butter
1/2 cup (30 g) corn syrup
1 oz. (25 g) finely chopped hazelnuts

1 Mix the crushed cookies with the melted butter and press the mixture into the bottom and half-way up the sides of an 8-in. (20-cm) springform cake pan. Chill 20 minutes until firm.

2 Pile alternate scoops of vanilla and chocolate ice cream over the cookie base, leaving the top quite rough. Freeze for at least 1 hour or until the ice cream is firm.

3 Meanwhile make the sauce. Place the chocolate, butter, and syrup in a bowl with 3 tbsp. water and melt slowly over a pan of gently simmering water. Stir until smooth then remove from the heat and let cool.

4 Toast the chopped hazelnuts under a preheated broiler until dark golden, 2 to 3 minutes.

5 Remove the ice cream pie from the pan. Pour the sauce over the ice cream then scatter with the hazelnuts. Freeze until you are ready to serve or serve straight away.

Fig and Ricotta Tart

This tart has a deliciously buttery shortbread base and is topped with creamy ricotta and fresh figs.

Serves 6–8

1¹/2 cups (175 g) all-purpose flour
generous 1/2 cup (80 g) ground rice
scant 1 cup (200 g) unsalted butter
scant ¹/2 cup (100 g) sugar

Filling

1 lb. 4 oz. (500 g) ricotta cheese
³/4 cup (75 g) confectioners' sugar
2 tsp. vanilla extract
6 ripe figs, quartered
2 tbsp. clear runny honey

1 Mix the flour and ground rice together. In a separate bowl, cream the butter and sugar together until light and fluffy. Mix in the flour and ground rice and bring together to form a ball.

2 Press the pastry into the bottom of a 9-in. (23-cm) loose-bottomed tart pan. Prick with a fork and chill 20 minutes.

3 Bake in a preheated oven 350°F (180°C, Gas 4) for 20 to 25 minutes. Let cool completely then remove from the tart pan.

4 To make the filling, beat the ricotta cheese with the confectioners' sugar and vanilla extract. Spread the mixture over the shortbread base. Arrange the figs over the ricotta. Drizzle with honey just before serving.

"The way to a man's heart is through his stomach."

Fanny Fern

Key Lime Pie

Traditionally made with the very tart Key limes from Florida, this fresh-tasting pie has a mousse-like filling and a delicious buttery crumb crust.

Serves 6–8

about 35 vanilla wafers
2–3 tbsp. sugar
1/3 cup (75 g) butter, melted
1 cup (250 ml) heavy cream, whipped, and finely grated lime peel, to decorate

Filling
8 oz. (225 g) sweetened condensed milk
1/2 cup (125 ml) lime juice
3 egg yolks

1 To make the crumb crust, put the wafers in a strong plastic bag and crush with a rolling pin until they form very fine crumbs. (Alternatively, use a food processor.) Mix the crumbs with the sugar and butter.

2 Pour the crumbs into a lightly greased 9-in. (23-cm) tart pan and, using the back of a spoon, press the crumbs evenly into the bottom and up the sides of the pan. Chill until firm.

3 To make the filling, whisk the condensed milk, lime juice, and egg yolks in a bowl until well blended and thickened. Pour into the crust and refrigerate until set.

4 Decorate with a little whipped cream and, if desired, lime peel. Serve with additional whipped cream.

THE HISTORY OF KEY LIME PIE

Key lime pie is one of America's most popular pies and the official dessert of the Key West area of Florida. The pie is available across America, with many diners and restaurants serving their own fantastically unique variations, as well as the original with its delicious custard-like lime filling.

The essential ingredient from which the pie takes its name is the small Key limes that were grown in the region in the 1850s and early 1900s. However, most Key limes actually come from Mexico today. They have a stronger and more acidic flavor than other limes, and are actually yellow when ripe, not green, giving the original pie its distinctive yellow color.

No-one knows who made the first Key lime pie, although it was created sometime in the late 1850s after the invention of sweetened condensed milk. Fresh milk was scarce in the Keys at that time because of the area's isolation and lack of cattle. The invention of canned milk was a real advantage to the Keys community and it was a natural step for this new product to be combined with the local fruit to create the luscious Key lime pie.

Eggnog Tart

An unusual tart that contains a good splash of Advocaat liqueur. You can serve it plain or decorate the top with fresh soft summer fruit.

Serves 6–8

2¼ cups (250 g) all-purpose flour
pinch of salt
⅓ cup (75 g) cold unsalted butter, diced
4 tbsp. (55 g) vegetable shortening
2–3 tbsp. cold water

Filling
4 eggs, separated
scant 1 cup (115 g) sugar
1 cup (250 ml) Advocaat liqueur
1¼ cups (300 ml) light cream
2 tsp. (10 g) powdered gelatin
soft fruit such as blackberries, raspberries, or strawberries, to decorate

1 Make the pastry following the instructions on pages 10–11, adding the vegetable shortening with the butter.

2 Roll out the pastry to line a 9-in. (23-cm) loose-bottomed tart pan. Prick the pastry and chill 10 minutes.

3 Line the pie shell with waxed paper and weigh down with baking beans. Bake in a preheated oven 375°F (190°C, Gas 5) for 20 minutes. Remove the paper and beans and cook another 5 minutes. Let cool completely.

4 To make the filling, beat the egg yolks with the sugar and liqueur. Bring the cream up to a boil in a nonstick saucepan. Pour the cream over the egg yolks and mix well. Return to the pan and stir over a gentle heat until the sauce thickens enough to coat the back of a spoon. Remove from the heat.

5 Place 4 tbsp. boiling water in a small bowl. Sprinkle over the gelatin and stir well until dissolved. Pour into the custard mixture and mix well. Let the custard cool then chill until thickened and on the point of setting.

6 Whisk the egg whites until they form stiff peaks and fold into the custard. Pour into the pastry case and level out. Chill for another 1/2 hour then decorate with soft fruit, if liked.

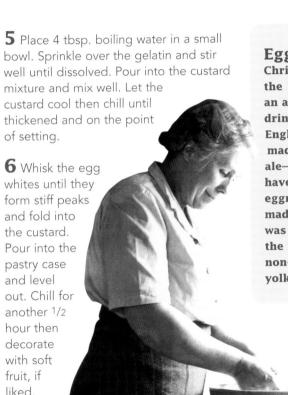

Eggnog has been a common Christmas drink in America since the 19th century, but it is actually an adaptation of older European drinks. In the 17th century, the English drank *posset*, a hot drink made of eggs, milk, and strong ale—often called *nog*—which may have been the forerunner to eggnog. However, a similar drink made with beer called *Biersuppe* was also served in Germany, and the French drank *Lait de Poule*, a non-alcoholic drink made of egg yolks, milk, and sugar.

Banoffee Tartlets

Slicing a whole pie can be a bit messy, so it makes sense to bake these delicious individual banana toffee tarts, especially when entertaining guests.

Makes 18

2 1/2 cups (275 g) all-purpose flour
pinch of salt
3/4 cup (175 g) unsalted butter, diced
2 egg yolks
4 tbsp. cold water

Filling
2/3 cup (150 g) butter
3/4 cup (175 g) sugar
14-oz. (400-g) can sweetened
  condensed milk
3 bananas
1 cup (250 ml) heavy cream, whipped

1 Make the pastry following the instructions on pages 10–11. Whisk the egg yolks with the cold water. Make a well in the center of the flour and pour in the egg mixture.

2 Divide the pastry into 18 pieces. Roll out each piece thinly on a lightly floured surface and use to line individual 2 1/2-in. (6-cm) tartlet pans. Let chill 20 minutes. Prick the bases and bake in a preheated oven 400°F (200°C, Gas 6), 10 minutes; let cool.

3 To make the filling, melt the butter and sugar in a pan. Pour in the milk. Cook, stirring constantly, until it comes to a boil. Lower the heat and simmer, stirring all the time, until the mixture thickens and turns a rich, golden brown. Remove from the heat.

4 Peel and slice two of the bananas and divide the slices among the tartlet pans. Pour the caramelized condensed milk over, filling each tartlet almost to the top and covering the bananas completely.

5 Let cool, then chill for about 1 hour to allow the filling to thicken. Pipe a swirl of whipped cream on each tartlet. Peel the remaining banana and slice it thinly. Cut each slice in half and arrange like butterfly wings on the cream. Serve at once.

Strawberry and Custard Tartlets

These individual custard-filled tarts topped with fresh strawberries make the perfect sensuous dessert to follow a romantic meal for two.

Makes 2

3/4 cup (100 g) all-purpose flour
4 tbsp. (55 g) butter
3 tbsp. confectioners' sugar
about 1 tbsp. water

Custard filling
2/3 cup (150 ml) milk
1 egg yolk
2 tbsp. sugar
2 tbsp. all-purpose flour

Topping
10–12 strawberries, hulled and halved
1 tbsp. strawberry jelly

1 Make the pastry following the instructions on pages 10–11, adding the confectioners' sugar with the flour and water.

2 Roll out the dough on a lightly floured surface and line two 3 1/2-in. (8-cm) tartlet pans. Prick the bases and chill 10 minutes.

3 Line the pie shell with waxed paper and weigh down with baking beans. Bake in a preheated oven 400°F (200°C, Gas 6), about 15 to 20 minutes. Remove the paper and beans and return to the oven until pale golden, 5 minutes. Let cool on a wire rack.

4 To make the custard filling, beat the milk, egg yolk, sugar, and flour in a bowl. Pour into a small saucepan and cook, stirring constantly until the mixture comes to a boil. Beat the custard until smooth, then simmer 2 minutes. Let cool, then spoon into the tartlet cases.

5 Arrange the strawberries on top of the custard. Gently heat the jelly and brush it over the strawberries. Let set a few minutes before serving.

Summer Berry Tart

This mixed berry tart is so pretty, and tastes simply divine. It's also immensely versatile, so you can experiment with different varieties of fruit depending on what is in season. Serve it with a spoonful of cream.

Serves 6–8

2¹/2 cups (275 g) all-purpose flour
4 tbsp. (25 g) confectioners' sugar
³/4 cup (175 g) unsalted butter, diced
2 egg yolks
4 tbsp. cold water
confectioners' sugar, for dusting

Filling
2¹/2 cups (600 ml) milk
4 egg yolks
¹/3 cup (75 g) sugar
¹/4 cup (25 g) all-purpose flour
¹/4 cup (25 g) cornstarch
grated peel of 1 orange

²/3 cup (150 ml) heavy cream
1 lb. (450 g) mixed summer berries such as raspberries, strawberries, blueberries, and redcurrants

1 Make the pastry following the instructions on pages 10–11, adding the confectioners' sugar with the flour. Whisk the egg yolks with the cold water. Make a well in the center of the flour and pour in the egg mixture. Continue to follow the method.

2 Roll out the pastry to line a 9¹/2-in. (24-cm) loose-bottomed tart pan. Prick the base and chill 10 minutes.

3 Line the pie shell with waxed paper and weigh down with baking beans. Bake in a preheated oven 375°F (190°C, Gas 5) until golden and crisp, 20 minutes. Remove the paper and beans and let cool on a wire rack.

4 To make the filling, pour the milk into a nonstick pan and bring to a boil. Mix the egg yolks with the sugar, and stir in the flour and cornstarch. Pour the mixture into the hot milk and mix well.

5 Bring the milk mixture to a boil, stirring continuously to prevent lumps forming. Once the custard is thick and smooth, remove from the heat and stir in the orange peel. Cover and chill.

6 Whip the cream to soft peaks then fold into the cold custard. Spoon the custard into the pastry case and level off. Arrange the mixed summer fruit over the custard and dust with confectioners' sugar before serving.

Soft delicious wild berries are wonderful throughout the summer. They are all great when eaten straight off the plant and on their own, but they make perfect pie fillings too. **The best loved of all the summer berries** in America and Britain is the delicate heart-shaped strawberry—the fruit of love and passion. In Florida, the delightful fruit has been celebrated at its own festival for nearly 70 years and who could possibly imagine the Wimbledon Tennis Championships without the traditional strawberries and cream?

"Strawberries, raspberries, and blackberries thrive here. From these they make a wonderful dish combined with syrup and sugar, which is called 'pai'. I can tell you that is something that glides easily down your throat; they also make the same sort of 'pai' out of apples or finely ground meat, with syrup added, and that is really the most superb."

Norwegian immigrant, Wisconsin, 1851

Orange Chiffon Pie

Ready-made chiffon pies became popular in the 1950s but making one from scratch is almost as quick and easy, as it needs no cooking at all. The *chiffon* filling comprises a gelatin mixture lightened with a meringue.

Serves 6–8

18–20 graham crackers, finely crushed
4 tbsp. (55 g) butter, melted
2 tbsp. sugar (optional)
julienne strips of orange peel,
    simmered in water until tender,
    to decorate
whipped cream, to serve

Filling
1/4 cup (60 ml) cold water
1 package or 1 tbsp. gelatin
4 eggs, separated

1 1/4 cups (275 g) sugar
grated peel of 1 orange
1/2 cup (125 ml) freshly squeezed
    orange juice
1/4 tsp. cream of tartar

1 To make the crumb crust, combine the crushed crackers, melted butter, and sugar, if using, in a large bowl. Pour the mixture into a 9-in. (23-cm) tart pan and, using the back of a spoon, press the crumbs into the bottom and up the sides. Chill until firm.

2 To make the filling, pour the water into a coffee cup or small bowl, sprinkle over the gelatin and let stand 10 minutes. Set the cup in a saucepan of just simmering water and heat gently, 5 minutes, stirring until the gelatin has completely dissolved.

3 Using a hand-held electric mixer, beat the egg yolks in a large heatproof bowl until light and fluffy, 1 to 2 minutes. Gradually beat in half the sugar, the grated orange peel, and juice.

4 Set the bowl over a saucepan of just simmering water (the bottom of the bowl should just touch the water) and cook, stirring constantly, until the mixture thickens and coats the back of a wooden spoon, 8 to 10 minutes.

5 Remove the bowl from the water, stir in the gelatin mixture and let cool, stirring occasionally.

6 Whisk the egg whites and cream of tartar in a large bowl until they form soft peaks. Gradually whisk in the remaining sugar until the whites are stiff and glossy.

7 Beat a spoonful of the whites into the cooled custard, then pour the custard mixture over the whites and fold together until they are just blended. Do not overwork the mixture—it does not matter if a few lumps of white remain.

8 Pour into the crumb crust, mounding the mixture in the middle, and chill until set, 4 to 6 hours.

9 Decorate with the julienne strips of orange peel and serve with whipped cream.

Covered & Double-Crust Pies

Deep-Dish Apple Pie à la Mode

Many 1950s housewives would bake over a dozen fruit pies a week. An ordinary, everyday pie, however, could achieve an instant air of sophistication by being served with a large scoop of ice cream, a style known as "à la mode." Try apricots, pears, plums, and cherries as an alternative to the apples.

1¹/₂ cups (175 g) all-purpose flour
¹/₂ tsp. salt
¹/₂ cup (120 g) butter
about ¹/₄ cup (60 ml) cold water
egg white or cream, for glazing

Filling
6 tart cooking apples, peeled, cored, and thinly sliced
1 tbsp. lemon juice
³/₄ cup (175 g) sugar, plus extra for sprinkling
¹/₄ cup (50 g) light brown sugar

2 tbsp. all-purpose flour
pinch of salt
¹/₄ tsp. freshly grated nutmeg
¹/₄ tsp. ground cinnamon
1 tbsp. butter

1 Make the pastry following the instructions on pages 10–11.

2 Divide the dough into two equal pieces. Roll out each one on a lightly floured surface into a circle about 11-in. (28-cm) diameter. Lay the first circle in the bottom of a deep 10-in. (25-cm) pie pan.

3 To make the filling, toss the apple slices in lemon juice to prevent them browning and arrange them closely together on top of the dough. In another bowl, mix together the two kinds of sugar, the flour, salt, nutmeg, cinnamon, and butter, and sprinkle the mixture over the apples.

4 Carefully lay the second pastry circle over the apples and press down the edges to seal. Trim off any excess pastry and decorate the edge with a fork, if desired. Make a couple of slashes in the top of the pie, or prick with a fork a couple of times to allow steam to escape. Brush the pastry lightly with whisked egg white or cream to glaze and sprinkle lightly with sugar, if liked.

5 Bake in a preheated oven 450°F (230°C, Gas 8) on the lowest shelf for 10 minutes, then reduce the temperature to 350°F (180°, Gas 4) and bake another 30 to 45 minutes. To brown the crust, move the pie to a higher shelf the last 10 minutes of baking. The apples are done when juice bubbles from the steam vents and the fruit feels tender when skewered.

6 Place the pie on a wire rack and let cool about 1 hour. Serve warm with your favorite flavor of ice cream.

The largest apple pie ever baked, according to Guinness World Records, weighed more than 34,000 pounds! It was made by the North Central Washington Museum at Walla Walla Point Park in 1997, in a dish that measured a massive 44 x 24 feet (13.4 x 7.3 metres). Three hundred volunteers were needed to core, peel, and slice all those apples before the pie could be baked in a huge and very strange-looking oven!

NATIONAL APPLE HARVEST FESTIVAL

The quintessential and most popular British and American pie is the traditional apple pie—a fact not forgotten by the organizers of the National Apple Harvest Festival. The apple pie baking and eating contests, and the pie auction, are some of the festival's best events and are an important part of its 40-year history.

There are apples galore at this fantastic harvest celebration that rejoices in all the history and traditions associated with the world's favorite fruit. The traditional apple bobbing and apple pie eating contests organized by children's entertainer Johnny Appleseed are hilarious events for the whole family to enjoy. The pie eating contest is far harder and messier than you'd expect—so it's just as much fun to watch as to compete in!

Black Currant and Apple Pie

An old-fashioned pie, with a hint of spice. Blackberries, cranberries, or red gooseberries can be used instead of black currants and are equally delicious.

Serves 6–8

2 1/2 cups (275 g) all-purpose flour
1/2 cup (55 g) confectioners' sugar
2/3 cup (150 g) butter
1 egg, plus 1 egg yolk
milk, for brushing
sugar, for sprinkling

Filling

3 tart cooking apples, peeled, cored, and thinly sliced
1 lb. 9 oz. (700 g) black currants, stripped from stalks
1 cup (225 g) sugar
1 tbsp. cornstarch
1/2 tsp. ground allspice
1/2 tsp. freshly grated nutmeg

1 Make the pastry following the instructions on pages 10–11, adding the confectioners' sugar with the flour. Add the whole egg and egg yolk and mix quickly to a rough dough. Wrap the dough and let rest in a cool place, but not the refrigerator for 20 minutes.

2 To make the filling, put the apple slices in a mixing bowl and add the black currants, sugar, cornstarch, allspice, and nutmeg. Toss gently to mix.

3 Roll out just under half of the pastry on a lightly floured surface to line a 10-in. (25-cm) pie pan. Spoon the filling into the pan. Roll out the remaining pastry on a lightly floured surface at least 1in. (2.5-cm) in diameter larger than the top of the pan.

4 Moisten the rim of the pie shell with water, then lift the pastry over the rolling pin and lay it on top of the filling. Press both pieces of pastry together on the rim and crimp the edges, if liked. Use any spare pastry to make decorative shapes for the top of the pie. Brush the top with milk, attach the shapes, then brush them with milk. Sprinkle the pastry with sugar.

5 Bake in a preheated oven 400°F (200°C, Gas 6) for 15 minutes.

6 Reduce the temperature to 350°F (180°C, Gas 4) and bake until golden, another 20 to 25 minutes. Serve warm.

There are hundreds of references in history, myth, and literature to **apples**: from Adam and Eve eating the forbidden fruit in the Garden of Eden to the golden apples in Greek and Roman mythology. Sir Isaac Newton is supposed to have thought up the law of gravity when he was hit on the head by an apple and William Tell became famous for shooting an apple off his son's head with a crossbow. John Chapman became an American folk hero as "Johnny Appleseed" because he spent forty-nine years in the American wilderness planting apple seeds.

Apple and Cinnamon Pie

Cinnamon is the best spice to add to a traditional apple pie. Resist the temptation to add other flavors that might overpower the delicious juicy taste of the apples.

Serves 6–8

2 cups (225 g) all-purpose flour
pinch of salt
1/2 cup (120 g) cold unsalted
   butter, diced
1/4 cup (55 g) sugar
2–3 tbsp. cold water
milk, for brushing

Filling
1/4–1/3 cup (55–75 g) sugar, plus extra
   for sprinkling
1 tsp. ground cinnamon
2 lb. 4 oz. (1 kg) dessert apples, peeled,
   cored, and thinly sliced

1 Make the pastry following the instructions on pages 10–11, adding the sugar after the butter has been rubbed in.

2 Divide the pastry into two pieces. Roll out one piece on a lightly floured surface into a 10-in. (25-cm) diameter circle and use to line a 9-in. (23-cm) pie pan.

3 Mix together the sugar and cinnamon, and sprinkle over the sliced apples. Arrange the apple slices in the pan—don't worry if the apples are above the top of the pan.

4 Roll out the remaining pastry into a 10-in. (25-cm) diameter circle. Brush the edge of the pastry in the pan with a little milk. Carefully lay the pastry over the apples and press down the edges to seal. Trim off any excess pastry and decorate the edge with a fork, if desired. Make two slashes in the top of the pie, or prick with a fork a couple of times.

5 Brush the top of the pastry with a little milk, then sprinkle with sugar. Bake in the center of a preheated oven 400°F (200°C, Gas 6) until the pastry is golden and the apples tender, 25 to 30 minutes. Serve warm or cold.

Lattice-Topped Linzertorte

This traditional Austrian tart has a rich and crumbly nut crust. It is filled with delicious fresh raspberries, rather than the typical raspberry jelly filling and is great served warm with heavy cream.

Serves 8

scant 1 cup (225 g) all-purpose flour
pinch of salt
1/3 cup (40 g) ground almonds
scant 1/2 cup (115 g) cold unsalted
  butter, diced
4 tbsp. light soft brown sugar
2 eggs, separated
3–4 tsp. cold water
confectioners' sugar, to decorate
heavy cream, to serve

Filling
1 lb. (450 g) raspberries
scant 1/2 cup (100 g) sugar
2 tsp. cornstarch mixed with 2 tsp.
  cold water
1 tbsp. lemon juice

1 Make the pastry following the instructions on pages 10–11, adding the almonds and brown sugar with the flour. Whisk the egg yolks with the cold water. Make a well in the center of the flour and pour in the egg mixture.

2 Roll out the pastry on a lightly floured surface and line a 8-in. (20-cm) loose-bottomed tart pan. Prick the base and chill 20 minutes. Reroll the trimmings with the remaining pastry. Cut into ten long strips, each 3/4-in. (2-cm) wide using a jagged pastry wheel.

3 To make the filling, cook the raspberries and sugar in a saucepan over low heat. Bring to a boil, stir in the cornstarch mixture and cook 2 minutes. Remove from the heat, stir in the lemon juice and let cool.

4 Spoon the raspberry mixture into the pie shell. Use the egg white to dampen the edges of the pastry, then lay the pastry strips over the top of the filling to make a lattice pattern. Lightly press the edges of the pastry together, and trim off any excess.

5 Put the tart on a preheated baking sheet and bake at 400°F (200°C, Gas 6) until golden, 20 to 25 minutes. Let cool 5 minutes. Remove from the pan and leave another 10 to 15 minutes. Dust with confectioners' sugar. Serve warm cut into wedges with cream.

The origins of this traditional lattice-topped tart are unclear, but it did come from the medieval Austrian town of Linz, hence its name **Linzertorte**—*torte* is the German word for cake. Some sources suggest it was invented in 1822 by a cook called Konrad Vogel, but others say that he simply rediscovered an old recipe in a cookbook from 1696. Linzertorte became very popular after it was brought to America in the 19th century and it has now inspired miniature, and even cookie, versions of itself—Linzer Tarts and Linzer Hearts.

Cranberry Pie

This single-crust pie couldn't be simpler to make—a true celebration of the fine flavor of cranberries, accentuated with fresh orange.

Serves 6

1¹/2 cups (175 g) all-purpose flour
pinch of salt
6 tbsp. (90 g) cold unsalted butter, diced
2 tbsp. sugar, plus extra for sprinkling
1 egg yolk
1–2 tbsp. milk

Filling
1¹/4 cups (275 g) sugar
finely grated peel and juice of 1 orange
1 lb. (450 g) cranberries

1 Make the pastry following the instructions on pages 10–11. Stir in the sugar following the butter, then add enough of the egg yolk to make a dough.

2 To make the filling, mix the sugar, orange peel, and juice in a bowl. Mix well, then stir in the cranberries. Spoon into a 6 cup (1.5 liter) deep pie pan.

3 Roll out the pastry on a lightly floured surface at least 1 in. (2.5 cm) diameter larger than the top of the pan. Cut off a 1–in. (2.5-cm) strip from around the edge.

4 Dampen the rim of the pie dish lightly with water and stick the pastry strip in place. Add the milk to any remaining egg yolk, and brush a little on the pastry strip. Fit the pastry round on the pie. Press the edges to seal and crimp with your fingers.

5 Decorate the top of the pie with pastry shapes, if liked. Cut one or two slits to allow steam to escape, then brush the pie with the remaining egg and milk mixture, and sprinkle with sugar.

6 Bake in a preheated oven 400°F (200°C, Gas 6) until the pastry is golden and crisp, 25 to 35 minutes. Sprinkle with more sugar before serving.

Old-Fashioned Peach and Raspberry Pies

These individual fruit pies bring a taste and aroma of summer into the kitchen. Perfect for picnics, packed lunches, or as a teatime treat.

Serves 4

2 cups (225 g) all-purpose flour
pinch of salt
1/2 cup (120 g) unsalted butter, diced
3–4 tbsp. cold water
1 tbsp. milk, for brushing
crème fraîche or sour cream, to serve

Filling
4 large ripe peaches, pitted and
  coarsely chopped
4 oz. (115 g) raspberries
1/3 cup (75 g) sugar, plus extra
  for sprinkling
juice of 1/2 lemon

1 Make the pastry following the instructions on pages 10–11.

2 Mix together the peaches, raspberries, sugar, and lemon juice and set aside.

3 Divide the pastry into four equal portions. Working with one portion at a time, divide into one-third and two-thirds. Roll out the larger piece to line a 4-in. (10-cm) individual pie pan. Fill with a quarter of the peach mixture.

4 Wet the edges of the pastry and then roll out the smaller portion of pastry. Use this pastry portion to top the pie, trimming off the excess and crimping the edges to seal. Snip a cross or hole in the top of the pie to allow steam to escape.

5 Brush the pastry top with a little milk and sprinkle with sugar. Repeat the process with the remaining three portions of pastry to make four pies.

6 Transfer the pies to the oven and bake in a preheated oven 400°F (200°C, Gas 6) until the pastry is golden and the fruit is tender, about 20 to 25 minutes.

7 Let cool about 10 minutes, then carefully turn the pies out of their pans. Serve with crème fraîche or sour cream.

Gooseberry Pie

Gooseberries have been becoming more popular in recent years and they make a wonderfully unusual pie filing. The delicious crumbly cornmeal pastry in this recipe complements the tart berries perfectly.

Serves 6

13/4 cups (200 g) all-purpose flour
1/2 cup (60 g) stone-ground cornmeal
pinch of salt
1/4 cup (50 g) light brown sugar
scant 2/3 cup (140 g) butter, diced
3–4 tbsp. cold water
1 egg, beaten
whipped cream or custard, to serve

Filling
1 lb. 9 oz. (700 g) gooseberries
4 tbsp. sugar, plus extra for dusting

1 Make the pastry following the instructions on pages 10–11, adding the cornmeal and brown sugar with the flour.

2 To make the filling, mix the gooseberries with 4 tbsp. of sugar.

3 Divide the pastry into two pieces, one slightly bigger than the other. Roll out the larger piece and use to line an 8-in. (20-cm) shallow pie pan. Spoon the gooseberries into the pan. Brush the rim of the pastry with a little beaten egg.

4 Roll out the remaining piece of pastry and lay it over the berries. Press down and seal the edges. Cut off any overhanging pastry and crimp the edges. Chill 20 minutes then brush the top with a little more egg and dust with sugar.

5 Bake in a preheated oven 375°F (190°C, Gas 5) until golden, 40 minutes. Serve warm with whipped cream or custard.

Cherry Pie

An all-time classic, use fresh pitted
black cherries, or if they are out of
season or you are short of time try
canned pitted cherries.

Serves 6–8

generous 3 cups (375 g) all-purpose flour
1/2 tsp. salt
3/4 cup (120 g) unsalted butter, diced
3/4 cup (120 g) vegetable shortening
2–3 tbsp. water
milk, for brushing

Filling

13/4 lb. (800 g) pitted fresh or canned
  cherries
1/4 cup (55 g) sugar, plus extra
  for dusting
2 tbsp. cornstarch
1/2 tsp. ground cinnamon
pinch of freshly grated nutmeg

1 Make the pastry following the
instructions on pages 10–11.

2 Roll out the pastry to line a deep
9-in. (23-cm) loose-bottomed tart pan.
Prick the pastry and chill 10 minutes.

3 Line the pie shell with waxed paper
and weigh down with baking beans. Bake
in a preheated oven 400°F (200°C, Gas 6)
until golden and crisp, 20 to 25 minutes.

4 Remove the paper and beans and
reduce the oven to 350°F (180°C, Gas 4).

5 To make the filling, mix the cherries
with the sugar, cornstarch, and spices.

6 Divide the pastry into two pieces, one
a little bigger than the other. Roll out the
larger piece of pastry and line an 8-in.
(20-cm) diameter x 11/2-in. (4-cm) deep

pie pan. Spoon the cherry mixture into the pie. Brush the edges of the pastry with a little milk.

7 Roll out the remaining piece of pastry and lay it over the cherries. Press down and seal the edges. Cut off any overhanging pastry and crimp the edges. Chill 20 minutes then brush the top with a little more milk and dust with sugar.

8 Bake in a preheated oven 350°F (180°C, Gas 4) until golden, about 45 minutes. Let stand 5 minutes before serving.

CHERRY PIE BAKING CONTEST

Cherry pies are an American favorite. A classic cherry pie with a delicious lattice crust is the pie of choice at every diner and truck stop. But this versatile dessert is great filled with any type of cherries and in all crusts—from double-crust to lattice, crumble to strudel, this classic fruit pie is a real winner!

1932 saw the first-ever National Cherry Pie Baking Contest, with the competitors bringing their winning recipes from regional events across the country. The contest became hugely popular in the 1950s, with more and more women wanting to take part.

The winner of the 21st contest in 1953—Maxine Walker from Alabama— was only 16 years old when she beat 47 other girls to win the coveted prize. She is pictured tasting her winning pie surrounded by fellow finalists Frances Evers, Zolfo Springs, Valerie Handley, and Dorothy Ann Beno.

Strawberry and Rhubarb Lattice Tart

Lattice tops are fun to make and far easier than most people expect. In this recipe, the pastry is woven on a board and then transfered to the pie once chilled to stop the fruit juices from soaking into it.

Serves 6–8

1 cup (120 g) all-purpose flour
pinch of salt
1/4 cup (60 g) cold unsalted butter, diced
1–2 tbsp. cold water
2 tbsp. sugar
milk, for brushing
2 tsp. turbinado sugar, for sprinkling

Filling
1 lb. (450 g) rhubarb, cut into chunks
1/3–1/2 cup (75–120 g) sugar, to taste
finely grated peel of 1 orange
1 1/2 tbsp. cornstarch or arrowroot
12 oz. (350 g) strawberries, hulled and halved, if large

1 Make the pastry following the instructions on pages 10–11, adding the sugar after the butter has been rubbed in.

2 Roll out one third of the pastry and line a 9-in (23-cm) loose-bottomed tart pan. Chill 10 minutes along with the remaining pastry until needed.

3 Put the rhubarb, 1/3 cup (75 g) of the sugar, and the orange peel in a saucepan over a gentle heat. Cook, stirring occasionally, until the rhubarb is tender and juicy, but still retains its shape, about 8 to 10 minutes. Taste for sweetness and add the remaining sugar, if necessary.

4 Mix the cornstarch with 1 tbsp. cold water until smooth. Stir into the rhubarb, return the mixture to a gentle simmer and cook 1 to 2 minutes until thickened. Remove from the heat and let cool. Stir in the strawberries.

5 Meanwhile, place a baking sheet on the center shelf of the oven and preheat to 400°F (200°C, Gas 6).

6 Remove the pastry-lined pan from the fridge. Line with waxed paper, weigh down with baking beans, and transfer to the oven. Bake 12 minutes.

7 Remove the paper and beans and return to the oven for another 10 minutes until golden and crisp. Let cool slightly.

8 Meanwhile, cut a large square of waxed paper and place on top of a chopping board or flat plate. Make room in the freezer for this.

9 Remove the remaining pastry from the fridge. Roll out the pastry on a lightly floured surface to make a large rectangle. Using a jagged pastry wheel, cut 10 to 12 long strips of pastry each about 1-in. (2.5-cm) wide.

10 On the prepared chopping board or plate, weave the strips of pastry into a lattice pattern, leaving a 1/2-in. (1-cm) gap between the strips.

11 When you have finished, transfer the board or plate to the freezer, 20 to 30 minutes. This will make it very easy to transfer to the filled tart pan.

12 Pour the rhubarb-strawberry mixture into the cooked pie shell. Brush the edges of the pastry with a little water or milk. Remove the lattice top from the freezer and arrange over the filling. Cut off any excess from the edges using the jagged pastry wheel and press the pastry to seal the edges all round.

13 Brush the pastry lightly with a little water or milk and sprinkle with the brown sugar. Transfer to the baking sheet in the oven and bake until the pastry is golden and the filling is bubbling, 30 to 35 minutes.

14 Let cool about 15 minutes in the pan then carefully remove and let cool for another 10 minutes before serving cut into wedges. Also delicious served cold.

Freeform
Pies

Almond Pithiviers

This classic pastry takes its name from the French town of Pithiviers and consists of two layers of light puff pastry with an almondy, custard filling.

Serves 8

12 oz. (350 g) ready-made puff pastry
1 egg, beaten
1 tbsp. confectioners' sugar, to decorate

Filling
1 cup (250 ml) milk
1 tsp. vanilla extract
3 egg yolks
1/4 cup (55 g) sugar
1 heaping tbsp. cornstarch
1/2 cup (120 g) unsalted butter, softened
scant 1/2 cup (100 g) sugar
1 cup (120 g) ground almonds

1 To make the filling, place the milk and vanilla extract in a saucepan and slowly bring to a boil. Mix the egg yolks with the sugar and cornstarch. Pour the boiling milk over the egg yolk mixture and stir well.

2 Return the mixture to the pan and cook over low heat, stirring constantly, until the custard has thickened, about 1 minute. Take off the heat and cover with plastic wrap to stop a skin from forming on the top; let cool.

3 Whisk the butter and sugar together until light and fluffy. Stir in the ground almonds then fold in the cold custard.

4 Divide the pastry into two pieces. Roll out one piece of pastry 1/8-in. (3-mm) thick and cut out a circle 10-in. (25-cm) in diameter. Place on a nonstick baking sheet and spread the almond mixture over the pastry, leaving a 1-in. (2.5-cm) margin around the edge. Brush the edge with beaten egg.

5 Roll out the second piece of pastry to the same thickness but 11-in. (28-cm) in diameter. Lay it over the almond topped pastry and press down to seal the edges. Chill 30 minutes.

6 Brush the surface with a little more beaten egg and score the top in a diamond pattern. Bake in a preheated oven 400°F (200°C, Gas 6), about 35 to 40 minutes. Let stand 5 minutes before dusting with confectioners' sugar and serving.

Most of the world's almonds are grown in California, and both Oakley and the Capay Valley celebrate this at their **Annual Almond Festivals**. These celebrations are great community get-togethers, which show the tremendous pride the Californian residents feel for their local crops. But they are great fun for visitors too! With events ranging from parades and fun-runs to almond cooking contests, there is something for everyone and all are welcome to join in the festivities.

Baklava

A favorite in the Middle East, Greece, and Turkey, this incredibly sweet dessert consists of layers of butter-drenched phyllo pastry with syrupy nuts—a little goes a long way.

Serves 8

2 cups (450 g) sugar
1 2/3 cups (400 ml) water
juice of 1 lemon
3/4 cups (175 g) unsalted butter, melted
12 oz. (350 g) phyllo pastry
1 1/4 cups (200 g) walnuts, very finely chopped
1 1/2 cups (230 g) unsalted pistachios, very finely chopped

1 Place the sugar in a large saucepan with the water and lemon juice. Dissolve the sugar over low heat then simmer until the syrup is quite thick and sticky, 20 to 25 minutes. Remove from the heat and let cool completely.

2 Brush a little melted butter over the bottom of a rectangular roasting pan, about 8 x 10-in. (20 x 25-cm). Place three layers of pastry in the pan, brushing each one with melted butter.

3 Mix the chopped nuts together and scatter a quarter of them over the pastry. Then spoon 2 to 3 tbsp. of the cooled sugar syrup over the top.

4 Layer another three sheets of pastry over the nuts, again brushing each layer with melted butter. Continue to layer with the nuts, syrup, and pastry. Finish with a layer of pastry and brush the top with melted butter.

5 Bake in a preheated oven 350°F (180°C, Gas 4) for 40 minutes. Remove from the oven, pour over any remaining sugar syrup and let cool completely. Serve cut into small squares.

THE HISTORY OF BAKLAVA

The exact origins of baklava are uncertain because Turkey, Greece, and the Middle East all had strong links to the dessert long before it reached America and Britain. It is believed that the earliest form of baklava was a dessert made up of layers of bread dough filled with nuts and honey, which was eaten by the wealthy Assyrians as early as the 8th century B.C.

The Greeks played their part in refining the dessert by creating a form of dough that could be rolled as thin as a leaf— phyllo pastry. Baklava then began to take on a life of its own as each country added its own local flavor and spices to the dessert as sailors and merchants brought it across its borders.

Baklava was finally perfected in the Turkish Empire in the 16th century as bakers and chefs from all over the region combined their local ingredients and refined their pastry-making techniques in the Turkish palaces. Baklava is now popular throughout the world, but Turkey has the reputation for making the best baklava using the finest layers of pastry and the aphrodisiacs walnut and honey as its principal ingredients.

"...I'd like the pie heated, and I don't want the ice cream on top. I want it on the side, and I'd like strawberry instead of vanilla if you have it. If not, then no ice cream, just whipped cream, but only if it's real, if it's out of a can, then nothing."

Meg Ryan as Sally Albright in
"When Harry Met Sally"

Freeform Spiced Plum Pie

Try to buy really plump, ripe plums for this recipe—it will give the best flavor to the pie. Serve with crème fraîche or whipped cream.

Serves 6–8

1/2 cup (75 g) pecans, very finely
    chopped
13/4 cups (200 g) all-purpose flour
2/3 cup (150 g) unsalted butter, diced
1/2 cup (125 ml) sour cream
crème fraîche or whipped cream,
    to serve

Filling
2 lb. (900 g) ripe plums, pitted
    and quartered
1/2 cup (100 g) light brown sugar
1 tsp. ground cinnamon
1/2 tsp. ground dried ginger
pinch of freshly grated nutmeg

1 To make the pastry, place the pecans, flour, and butter in a food processor and process briefly until it forms very coarse bread crumbs. Add the sour cream and process for another 4 to 5 seconds.

2 Turn the pastry out onto a lightly floured board and bring the mixture together with your hands. Wrap in plastic wrap and chill 20 minutes.

3 To make the filling, place the plums in a bowl and mix with the brown sugar and spices.

4 Roll out the pastry on a lightly floured surface into a circle 14-in. (35-cm) in diameter and place on a nonstick baking sheet. Pile the plums in the center of the pastry, leaving a 3-in. (7.5-cm) margin.

5 Bring up the sides of the pastry to half cover the plums. Let chill 20 minutes then bake in a preheated oven 400°F (200°C, Gas 6) for 40 to 45 minutes. Serve with crème fraîche or whipped cream.

Spiced Apple and Mincemeat Pie

This is similar to a strudel but easier to assemble! Serve warm with a spoonful of vanilla ice cream.

Serves 4–6

2 lb. 4 oz. (1 kg) tart cooking apples, peeled, cored, quartered, and thinly sliced
1/3 cup (70 g) soft brown sugar
1 tsp. ground allspice
5 oz. (150 g) good quality mincemeat
5 oz. (150 g) phyllo pastry
1/3 cup (75 g) butter, melted
confectioners' sugar, to decorate

1 Mix the apples with the brown sugar, allspice, and mincemeat.

2 Lay one layer of phyllo pastry, about 11 x 12-in. (28 x 30-cm) on a nonstick baking sheet. Brush with a little of the melted butter and cover with a second layer of pastry. Brush this layer with a little more butter.

3 Pile the apples in the center of the pastry, leaving a margin about 2-in. (5-cm) around the edge. Fold up the sides of the pastry around the apples. Place another layer of pastry over the top and tuck in the edges. Brush with melted butter. Repeat until all the pastry is used.

4 Place in a preheated oven 400°F (200°C, Gas 6) and bake until golden, 40 minutes. Let stand 10 minutes, then dust with confectioners' sugar and serve.

Tarte Tatin

A French classic, this upside-down tart looks spectacular and is very easy to make if you use ready-made puff pastry. Other types of fruit can be used—pears, plums, nectarines, and apricots work well, as does rhubarb.

Serves 8

10 oz. (275 g) ready-made puff pastry,
 thawed if frozen
whipped cream or ice cream, to serve

Filling
6 dessert apples,
1 tbsp. lemon juice
6 tbsp. (90 g) butter
6 tbsp. sugar

1 To make the topping, slice the apples into quarters. Remove the core and peel from each quarter, then use a fork to score the rounded side. Cut each quarter in half widthwise, then toss the pieces in the lemon juice.

2 Melt the butter in a 9-in. (23-cm) heavy-bottomed, ovenproof skillet. Stir in the sugar until it has melted then remove from the heat.

3 Arrange the apple quarters, scored-side-down, in concentric circles in the pan, packing them quite tightly together. Put the pan over low heat and cook gently, without disturbing the apples, until they begin to caramelize, about 15 minutes.

4 Preheat the oven to 400°F (200°C, Gas 6). Roll out the puff pastry on a lightly floured surface to a circle slightly larger than the top of the skillet. Wrap the pastry over the rolling pin, then carefully place it on top of the apples—taking care not to burn your fingers, carefully tuck the edges inside the skillet.

5 Transfer to the oven and bake until the pastry has risen well and is golden brown, 20 to 25 minutes.

6 Let the tart cool 5 minutes, then gently ease a knife between the top crust and the pan. Place a plate on top, then carefully invert so that the apples are now on top. Serve warm with whipped cream or ice cream.

Tarte Tatin **was invented by accident** in the late 1800s by French hotel-owners Stephanie and Caroline Tatin. While cooking apple tart for their guests, the sisters accidentally put the apple filling in the oven without the pastry. They tried to save the meal by adding more butter and sugar to the apples and by putting the pastry on top. They turned the tart over and served it hot with the caramelized apples on top. Their tart was a great success with their guests and quickly became popular all over France.

THE PILLSBURY BAKE-OFF CONTEST

In 1949, Pillsbury held its first ever "Grand National Recipe and Baking Contest" in New York City to celebrate its 80th anniversary. One hundred amateur cooks competed in the final at the Waldorf Astoria Hotel, sharing their finest and most original recipes. The event was an immediate success and quickly became an American Institution—it is now held every other year as the "Pillsbury Bake-Off Contest."

Classic pie recipes have always been popular at the contest. A great apple pie has a timeless appeal that has made it a favorite throughout the contest's history. In 1962, Julia Smoger of Iowa won the contest with her unique "Apple Pie '63." She is pictured being presented with her $25,000 prize by the former First Lady Mamie Eisenhower while the other judges enjoy another taste of the delicious winning pie.

Tarte Fine Aux Pommes

A classic—this delightful French apple tart is simple to make, but looks impressive nevertheless.

Serves 4

12 oz. (350 g) ready-made puff pastry
butter, for greasing
2 dessert apples, cored, halved, and
   thinly sliced lengthwise
1^1/$_2$ tbsp. confectioners' sugar
2 tbsp. apricot jelly
light cream, to serve

1 Roll out the pastry thinly and cut a 9-in. (23-cm) circle. Transfer to a lightly greased baking sheet.

2 Lay the apple slices on the pastry in concentric circles, overlapping slightly and leaving a ^{1}/$_2$-in. (1-cm) margin around the edge. Dust generously with confectioners' sugar.

3 Transfer the baking sheet to a preheated oven 375°F (190°C, Gas 5) and bake until the pastry is risen and the apples are tender and golden at the edges, 20 to 25 minutes.

4 Gently heat the apricot jelly in a small saucepan, then press through a strainer to remove any large pieces. Brush the warm jelly generously over the hot apple tart to glaze. Let cool slightly and serve warm with cold cream.

Summer Berry Galette

This freeform French puff pastry tart is an attractive, simple dessert that uses the freshest summer fruit. Delicious with single cream.

Serves 6

1 lb. (450 g) ready-made puff pastry

Filling
6 oz. (175 g) strawberries, hulled
    and sliced
4 oz. (115 g) raspberries
5 oz. (150 g) blueberries
1/4 cup (25 g) confectioners' sugar
1/3 cup (40 g) ground almonds

1 Roll out the pastry on a lightly floured surface and cut a circle 10-in. (25-cm) in diameter. Place on a baking sheet and chill, 20 minutes.

2 To make the filling, mix all the fruit together and stir in the confectioners' sugar. Sprinkle the ground almonds over the pastry and scatter the fruit on top, leaving a 1/2-in. (1-cm) margin around the edge.

3 Cook in a preheated oven 400°F (200°C, Gas 6) until the pastry is golden, 20 minutes. Let stand a minute or two before serving.

Upside-Down Pear Tart with Cardamom

This is an alternative to the classic apple *tarte Tatin* made with pears. Cardamom is a surprisingly effective flavor with this popular fruit.

Serves 4–6

10 oz. (275 g) ready-made puff pastry
sour cream, to serve

Filling
1/2 cup (120 g) sugar
3–4 tbsp. cold water
about 10 green cardamom pods, seeds
   removed and crushed
4–6 ripe but firm pears, depending on
   size, cored and quartered lengthwise
4 tbsp. (55 g) unsalted butter, diced

1 To make the filling, put the sugar and water in a 9-in. (23-cm) heavy-bottomed, ovenproof skillet. Stir over a low heat until the sugar has dissolved completely. Increase the heat and bring the mixture to a rapid simmer.

2 As soon as the sugar begins to color, sprinkle over the cardamom seeds—do not stir. Carefully arrange the pear quarters in concentric circles in the skillet. Tilt and turn the skillet often until the sugar bubbling up between the pears is deep brown and smells nutty. Immediately remove from the heat and add butter wherever there are spaces between the fruit. Let cool about 20 minutes.

3 Roll out the puff pastry thinly then cut a circle about 1-in. (2.5-cm) larger than the diameter of the skillet. Carefully lay the pastry over the pears, tucking it down the sides of the pan to enclose the fruit.

4 Transfer the skillet to a preheated oven 400°F (200°C, Gas 6) and bake until the pastry is risen and golden, 25 minutes.

5 Remove from the oven and let stand about 10 minutes before carefully inverting onto a serving plate. Serve warm, cut into wedges, with sour cream.

Apricot and Banana Crumble

A great favorite with the whole family, this warming and satisfying dessert is also simple to make. It is just as delicious served with custard or cream.

Serves 4–6

9 oz. (250 g) dried apricots
1 cup (250 ml) fresh orange juice
4 bananas
1/4 tsp. ground cinnamon
1/4 tsp. ground dried ginger

Topping
13/4 cups (200 g) all-purpose flour
generous 1/2 cup (115 g) light
 brown sugar
1/2 cup (120 g) unsalted butter

1 Soak the apricots in the orange juice for 2 hours until they have plumped up.

2 Carefully slice the bananas into 1/2-in. (1-cm) rounds and mix with the apricots and the spices. Place in an ovenproof dish.

3 To make the topping, mix the flour with the brown sugar and rub in the butter until it forms coarse bread crumbs. Then sprinkle the mixture over the fruit.

4 Cook in a preheated oven 400°F (200°C, Gas 6) until golden, 35 to 40 minutes. Serve warm with chilled light cream or custard.

Cherry Cinnamon Cobbler

This traditional warming pudding is topped with a thick scone-like crust, perfect fuel for a cold winter's day.

Serves 6

2 lb. 4 oz. (1 kg) pitted black cherries in heavy syrup
2 oz. (50 g) dried cherries
1/2 cup (100 g) light brown sugar
2 tbsp. cornstarch

Topping
13/4 cups (200 g) all-purpose flour
pinch of salt
2 tsp. baking powder
1 tsp. ground cinnamon
1/2 cup (100 g) soft brown sugar
generous 1/3 cup (85 g) butter, melted
1/2 cup (125 ml) milk

1 Drain the cherries, reserving the syrup. Place them with the dried cherries in a large pie pan. Place the syrup (about 2 1/2 cups (600 ml)) in a saucepan and add the brown sugar. Slowly bring to a boil, stirring until the sugar has dissolved.

2 Mix the cornstarch with a little water and stir into the syrup. Cook until the syrup thickens, 1 to 2 minutes, and pour the syrup over the cherries.

3 To make the topping, combine the flour, salt, baking powder, cinnamon, and sugar in a bowl. Stir in the melted butter and milk and mix well. Spoon dollops of the batter over the cherries.

4 Bake in a preheated oven 375°F (190°C, Gas 5) until the topping is risen and golden, 35 to 40 minutes.

Cherry Strudel

Soft and luscious, this traditional favorite will be an instant hit with all the family. The cherries must be dark and ripe for the best flavor—you could use canned cherries but make sure they are well drained. If you don't have a homemade sponge, a store-bought Madeira cake is ideal for the cake crumbs.

Serves 8

4 large sheets phyllo pastry
4 tbsp. (55 g) unsalted butter, melted
confectioners' sugar, for dusting

Filling
1 lb. 4 oz. (550 g) fresh black cherries, pitted and halved
1/4 cup (30 g) ground almonds
1/3 cup (75 g) sugar
1 cup (55 g) fresh cake crumbs

1 To make the filling, place the black cherries in a bowl with the ground almonds, sugar, and cake crumbs, then stir to combine.

2 Cover the phyllo pastry with a damp cloth to prevent it drying out. Lay a sheet of the pastry on a large flat baking sheet and brush with a little melted butter. Lay a second sheet over the top and brush with butter. Repeat this twice more so you have a rectangle of four sheets of pastry.

3 Spoon the cherry mixture over the top, leaving a 2-in. (5-cm) margin around the edge. Roll up the longest side—like you would a jelly roll. Tuck in the ends and form into a horseshoe shape.

4 Brush the surface of the pastry with more butter and bake in a preheated oven, 375°F (190°C, Gas 5), about 25 minutes. Dust with confectioners' sugar and serve warm or at room temperature.

MICHIGAN NATIONAL CHERRY FESTIVAL

America is the leading producer of sweet and sour cherries in the world, and Michigan grows about 75% of the American sour cherry crop—around 250 million pounds of cherries every year! Traverse City, Michigan calls itself the "Cherry Capital of the World" and cherry trees have flourished in the area since 1852. The city now holds the ultimate celebration of the tiny ruby-red fruit at its annual Cherry Festival.

The festival began in 1925 as the "Blessing of the Blossoms"— a traditional spring ceremony at which local cherry farmers and pastors would come together to bless the fruit crop. It is now a huge National festival, with thousands of visitors coming from all over the world to join in the weeklong celebrations along the shores of beautiful Lake Michigan.

There is no excuse for being hungry at the festival because cherry pie eating contests and cherry pit spitting contests are held nearly every day! If this is a little too messy for you, there are plenty of other chances to eat as many cherries as you can, such as the Taste of Cherries Food Fair and the Very Cherry Luncheon. You can also eat all the cherries you can pick on the more traditional orchard tours!

Rhubarb and Custard Puff Pie

A delicious puff pastry pie oozing with custard and fruit filling.

Serves 4–6

13 oz. (375 g) ready-made puff pastry
1 egg, beaten
1/4 cup (25 g) confectioners' sugar, for dusting

Filling
13 oz. (375 g) young rhubarb, cut into 2-in. (5-cm) pieces
1/3 cup (75 g) sugar
1 1/4 cups (300 ml) ready-made custard
1 tsp. vanilla extract

1 Place the rhubarb in an ovenproof dish and sprinkle over the sugar. Cover and cook in a preheated oven 350°F (180°C, Gas 4) until tender, 40 minutes. Let cool.

2 Mix the custard with the vanilla extract and carefully stir in the rhubarb, being careful not to break up the fruit.

3 Roll out the pastry on a lightly floured surface to form a 12 x 15-in. (30 x 38-cm) rectangle and place on a nonstick baking sheet. Pile the custard and rhubarb onto one half leaving a 1-in. (2.5-cm) margin around the edge. Brush the margin with a little of the beaten egg.

4 Fold the pastry half over the filling and press down to seal the edges—crimp with your fingers or the back of a fork. Brush the top with a little more egg. Sift the sugar evenly over the top.

5 Cook the pie in a preheated oven 350°F (180°C, Gas 5) until risen and golden, 25 to 30 minutes. Let stand 5 minutes before serving.

Freeform Strawberry Rhubarb Pie

Strawberries and rhubarb combine perfectly in this recipe, with neither fruit overpowering the other, to give the pie a deliciously subtle flavor.

Serves 4–6

generous 1 cup (120 g) all-purpose flour
pinch of salt
1/3 cup (75 g) butter, diced
1/2 cup (60 g) ground almonds
1/4 cup (55 g) sugar
3–4 tbsp. cold water

Filling
1 lb. (450 g) rhubarb, cut into chunks
1/3–1/2 cup (75–120 g) sugar, to taste
1 vanilla bean
2 strips lemon peel
2 tsp. cornstarch or arrowroot
12 oz. (350 g) strawberries, hulled and halved if large
2 tsp. coarse sugar

1 Make the pastry following the instructions on pages 10–11, adding the ground almonds and sugar to the rubbed in mixture. You may need a little extra water to bind this pastry.

2 To make the filling, put the rhubarb, 1/3 cup sugar, vanilla bean, and lemon peel into a saucepan over a gentle heat.

3 Cook, stirring often, until the rhubarb is tender and quite juicy but still holding its shape, about 8 to 10 minutes. Taste for sweetness and add the remaining sugar if necessary.

4 Mix the cornstarch with a little water until smooth. Stir into the rhubarb, then return to a gentle simmer. Cook until thickened, 1 to 2 minutes.

5 Remove from the heat and stir in the strawberries. Set aside until cold. Remove the vanilla bean and lemon peel.

6 Roll out the pastry to a large circle about 15-in. (37-cm) in diameter. Transfer to a large, nonstick baking sheet.

7 Spoon the cold strawberry-rhubarb mixture into the center of the pastry and gather the pastry around the filling, leaving an open top. Brush the pastry with a little cold water and sprinkle with the coarse sugar.

8 Transfer the baking sheet to the center of a preheated oven 400°F (200°C, Gas 6) and bake, about 20 to 25 minutes. Let cool then serve cut into wedges.

Although **rhubarb was being used as a medicine** in China over 4,000 years ago, its use in cooking is relatively recent. It was grown in Britain in the 16th century as an ornamental plant, but people in Britain and America only started using sweetened rhubarb in their pies, puddings, and jellies in the early 19th century. Rhubarb may not be one of the world's most popular fruits (actually, it's a vegetable), but it certainly makes a great pie filling!

Glossary

The following culinary terms will provide useful guidelines for international readers to follow.

U.S.	British	U.S.	British
all-purpose flour	plain flour	pie shell	pastry case
almond extract	almond essence	pitcher	jug
beat	whisk	phyllo pastry	filo pastry
bittersweet chocolate	plain chocolate	plastic wrap	cling film
brioche pans	brioche tins	turbinado sugar	demerara sugar
confectioners' sugar	icing sugar	shredded coconut	desiccated coconut
cornstarch	cornflour	skillet	frying pan
dessert apples	eating apples	slivered almonds	flaked almonds
graham crackers	digestive biscuits	stone-ground cornmeal	fine polenta
heavy cream	double cream	sugar	caster sugar
jelly	jam	tart pan	flan tin
jelly roll	Swiss roll	vanilla bean	vanilla pod
light corn syrup	golden syrup	vanilla extract	vanilla essence
light cream	single cream	vanilla wafers	langue de chat bicuits
pan	tin	waxed paper	baking parchment
peel	zest		

Picture Credits

Pages 12, 15, 23, 27, 31, 33, 36, 39, 41, 53, 58, 62, 66, 71, 79, 85, 87, 90,107 © Getty Images. Cover, title page, pages 6, 18, 69 © Lambert/Getty Images. Page 48 © Gene Lester/Getty Images. Page 74 © Camerique/Getty Images. Page 102 © Dorothy Roberts Mac Leod/Getty Images. Pages 80, 96 © Bettmann/CORBIS.

Index